A Special Gift

FOR

_____

FROM

_____

DATE

_____

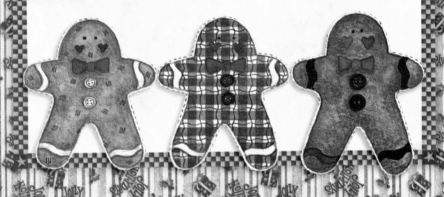

Introduction

The warmth of friends and family, the light in a child's eyes, festive decorations and twinkling lights are all a part of the excitement and wonder of the Christmas season. Nothing else brings out the good in people quite like Christmas. Whether it's leaving a gift for your postal carrier or putting a wreath on your car, there are so many little things you can do to give another person a reason to smile.

This little book contains lots of ideas to help you spread good cheer to others, but feel free to experiment and add your own variations to the list. Anything that brings joy to another can't be all that bad. And after all, isn't that what the season is all about?

So go on now and have yourself a merry little Christmas.

Have Yourself A Merry Little CHRISTMAS

Illustrated by DEBBIE MUMM
Written by BONNIE JENSEN

Brownlow

Start a snowball fight. No snow?
Start a water fight and remind
everyone that
it is the liquid
form of snow.

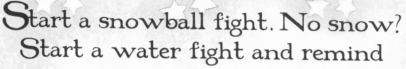

MERRY LITTLE VARIATION:

A pillow fight will do
in a pinch. Avoid
fireplaces and Christmas
trees—make it more
festive by using those
decorative little
Christmas pillows.

Let It Snow!
Let It Snow!
Let It Snow!

Visit a toy store
(even if you don't
have a legitimate reason to).
See if your favorite
childhood toy is still being
made, no matter how
strange it might appear
in its modern form.

MERRY LITTLE VARIATION:

Skip through the aisles of a toy store...
(run if you can remember how excited
you really were as a child).

Choose a gift for an underprivileged child. Nearly every mall in the country has an angel tree filled with giving opportunities.

MERRY LITTLE VARIATION:

Select two children who will have a nicer Christmas because of your gift-giving, and instantly double that wonderful feeling inside.

BIRD
SEED

Volunteer to read for children at your local library during the holiday season. Choose your favorite Christmas book or share a story from your childhood memories.

MERRY LITTLE VARIATION:

Bring a red sack filled with goodies to hand out to the children after they've been quiet and attentive for story time (those little candy canes will do). Enjoy being completely tickled inside.

I heard a bird sing in the dark of December
A magical thing and sweet to remember.
OLIVER HERFORD

Be a good neighbor.
Make a hot chocolate mix or bake them a little something and deliver it with a big smile.

MERRY LITTLE VARIATION:

Go the extra mile and add a coupon for one lawn mowing or leaf raking during the appropriate season—redeemable on the day of their choice.

Easy Homemade Hot Cocoa Mix:

2 c. instant nonfat dry milk powder

2 c. miniature marshmallows ★ c. confectioner's sugar

c. powdered nondairy creamer ★ c. semisweet chocolate chips

c. unsweetened cocoa ★ 1/3 c. sweetened ground cocoa

Stir all ingredients together until thoroughly blended. Pour the mix into a clear jar and tie a ribbon around the top for the perfect neighborly gift.

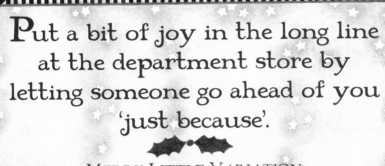

Put a bit of joy in the long line at the department store by letting someone go ahead of you 'just because'.

MERRY LITTLE VARIATION:

Put a lot of joy in the long line at the department store by letting everybody go ahead of you.

Think of it as a valuable lesson in kindness and patience.

Make this season a time of shopping for ways to give~ and have yourself the Merriest Little Christmas ever...

JOLLY HOLLYDAYS

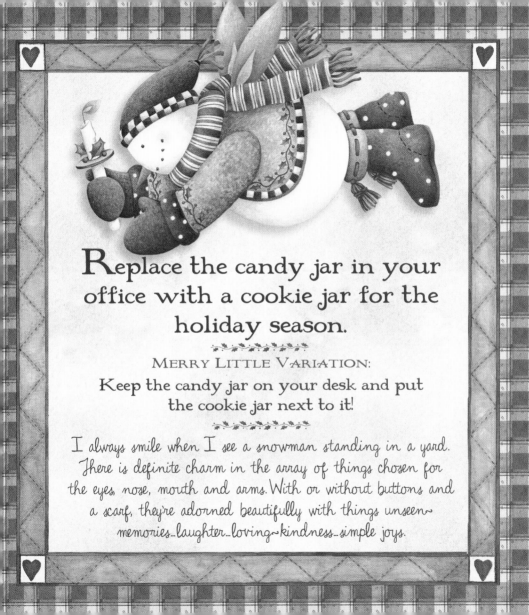

Replace the candy jar in your office with a cookie jar for the holiday season.

MERRY LITTLE VARIATION:
Keep the candy jar on your desk and put the cookie jar next to it!

I always smile when I see a snowman standing in a yard. There is definite charm in the array of things chosen for the eyes, nose, mouth and arms. With or without buttons and a scarf, they're adorned beautifully with things unseen~ memories...laughter...loving~kindness...simple joys.

Call the senior care center in your community to get a list of residents who don't receive mail on a regular basis. Send them each a Christmas card!

MERRY LITTLE VARIATION:

Hand-deliver the cards and enjoy firsthand their tender smiles and warm hearts.

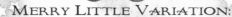

"Glory to God in the highest, and on earth peace, good will to men."

LUKE 2:14

Get together one and all
Watch the gentle snowflakes fall,
Scoop 'em, roll 'em, stack 'em tall
Have yourself a snowman's ball.

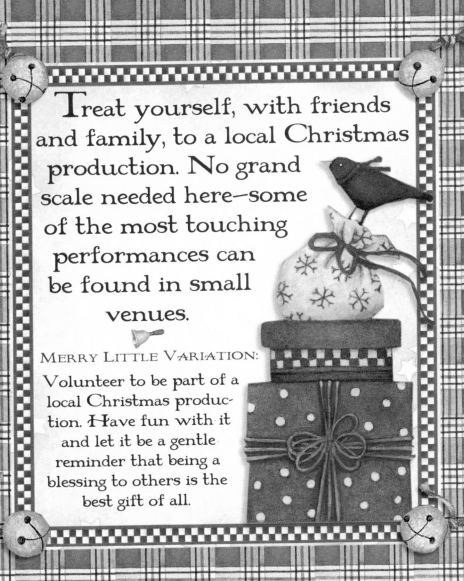

Treat yourself, with friends and family, to a local Christmas production. No grand scale needed here—some of the most touching performances can be found in small venues.

MERRY LITTLE VARIATION:

Volunteer to be part of a local Christmas production. Have fun with it and let it be a gentle reminder that being a blessing to others is the best gift of all.

Decorate your car! Tie a wreath to the front, put ribbons on the antenna, hang mistletoe from the rearview mirror...

MERRY LITTLE VARIATION:

...fill the back window with battery operated lights, stick those window adhesive cut-out things here and there, roll down the windows and play your favorite Christmas music really loud, (now you're getting the idea).

"To every thing there is a season, and a time to every purpose under the heaven."
ECCLESIASTES 3:1 KJV

Throw a "Kick-off the Christmas Season" party for your family and friends. Watch a classic holiday cartoon and follow it with "It's a Wonderful Life" or any other heartwarming movie of your choice. Serve popcorn, peanuts, cookies and hot cocoa.

MERRY LITTLE VARIATION:

Ask each of your guests to bring an exchange gift from the dollar store and go on a brief caroling expedition to your neighbors— then invite them to the party!

Fill your mailbox with candy for the mail carrier on Christmas Eve. Bundle it up so it's easy to remove and don't forget to add a thankful-for-you note.

MERRY LITTLE VARIATION:

If you know your mail carrier's schedule (and you probably do), make sure to peek out the window when they discover your 'sweet' surprise. Watching someone's face light up is incredibly festive.

Make an old-fashioned popcorn string for your Christmas tree.

MERRY LITTLE VARIATION: Make the string more jolly by using the bright colored popcorn, or by adding multi-colored gum drops in between the popcorn pieces. Be sure to follow the golden rule: eat a piece...string a piece...eat a piece...string a piece.

BIRD SEED

Go ice-skating. Be it rink, pond, river, or lake there's bound to be someplace you can go to take part in this wintry activity.

MERRY LITTLE VARIATION:

Take a whole bunch of children along (or adults who are willing to act like children). Lots of laughter and falling down adds to the overall joy of the experience.

I have come that they might have life, and that they might have it more abundantly.

JOHN 10:10

Have a glass of eggnog,
just because
it's Christmastime.

MERRY LITTLE VARIATION:

Fill your glass halfway
with eggnog and add
vanilla ice cream until
it reaches the top.
Crown it with
whipped cream.
Try to remember
why you ever
avoided this
holiday treat.

Make paper snowflakes. Fold a letter-size sheet into quarters and cut out every shape you can think of. Open. Voila!

MERRY LITTLE VARIATION:

Display your handiwork on a desktop Christmas tree and add some styrofoam 'snow-balls' to complete the ensemble.

Take a tour of lights around your town, city, suburb or countryside. Marvel at the creativity you never knew existed right there in your community.

MERRY LITTLE VARIATION:

Make a contest out of your tour. Choose the most impressive light display you see, take note of the address, and send them a "You Lit Up My Life" award. They'll be honored that you appreciated their time and effort.

Leave anonymous
"Happy Holiday" notes
for family, friends, co-workers,
pets. Include a compliment
or encouragement in each one
to make them feel special.

MERRY LITTLE VARIATION:

Think about adding more than words to
your anonymous notes...like dollar bills,
candy, or gift certificates for movie rentals.

M̲ake one of those cute, laminated Christmas ornaments with your picture in the middle and give it to your mom.

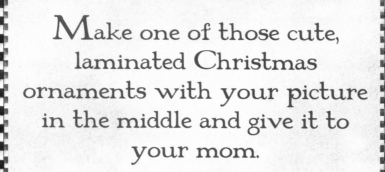

MERRY LITTLE VARIATION:

G̲ive your mom some extra hugs this Christmas and tell her you'll never outgrow the joy of having the best mom in the world.

Her children arise and call her blessed;
her husband also,
and he praises her.

PROVERBS 31:28